# Stoicism

## A Beginner's Guide to the Ancient Art, History, and Wisdom of the Stoic Philosophy

Elizabeth Nash

# Table of Contents

# Introduction

When most people hear the word "Stoic," they think of someone who is unfeeling or lacks emotion. This is actually the modern perception of what Stoicism is about. The original Stoic was much more than this. In this book, *"Stoicism: A Beginner's Guide to the Ancient Art, History, and Wisdom of the Stoic Philosophy,"* you will learn what Stoicism is really about.

Stoicism is actually an ancient Greek philosophy that dates back to around 300 B.C. and was initially developed by Zeno of Citium. The essence of the Stoic philosophy is one of using grit and self-control as ways of overcoming destructive emotions. This does not mean that a stoic seeks to eliminate all kinds of feelings from their life. The goal, rather, is to transform their emotions by avoiding what we would call 'worldly pleasures.' By doing so, a person is able to develop inner calm, better judgment, and freedom from unnecessary suffering.

This book is written for those people who are not yet fully familiar with the philosophy of Stoicism and are seeking to learn more about it. The book starts off with an overview of Stoicism, its origins, and how it gradually spread and developed. You will be able to learn the impact that Stoicism has had on various cultures throughout Europe and all over the world.

Like all other philosophies, Stoicism is founded on specific principles and doctrines. These philosophies have been used by many throughout history to improve their lives and those of others around them. The book covers all the basic tenets of Stoicism as well as the historical figures that made it famous.

You will also learn about some of the famous modern-day Stoics who are currently the movers and shakers of the world stage. You will be surprised to discover just how big of an impact this philosophy has had so far.

Stoicism has a lot of benefits, and you will learn how to adopt specific Stoic philosophies in different areas of your life. You can use these principles to learn how to have greater emotional control, especially over negative feelings like fear, anxiety, grief, and anger. Without a doubt, Stoicism can enhance the quality of your relationships.

Whether you are struggling how to handle failure or success, a Stoic approach has the potential of leading you down the right path. This is one philosophy that is not just theoretical in nature. It is something that you learn to adopt into your everyday life, and it is even more relevant in today's chaotic and overemotional world.

Maybe you are seeking a happier and more focused life. Why don't you try Stoicism? Take the time to read through this inspiring, relevant, and informative book. You may be surprised at how Stoicism may change your life for the better!

Thank you very much for choosing to for order this book.

Enjoy your reading!

direct or indirect, which are incurred as a result of the use of information contained within this document, including, but not limited to, —errors, omissions, or inaccuracies.

# Chapter 1:

# Unwrapping the Stoic Philosophy

What is your life like right now?

Are you satisfied with what you have, or do you look around you and wish you had what others possess? Do you always find yourself succumbing to fleeting temptations and following your emotions without really using clear judgment or thinking about the consequences? How's that working out for you so far?

In this chapter, we are going to open up this Pandora's box called Stoicism and try to figure it out. Stoicism is not just a set of beliefs that you mentally cram into your head and only use when you want to impress your friends. It is a way of life that you practice day in and day out. It incorporates logic, self-dialogue, and meditation designed to keep your focus fixed on the present moment.

## *Stoicism Defined*

What is the one thing that all human beings crave? The majority would mention happiness, and they would be right. We all crave a life where we are happy and free from all the stresses and cares of this hectic world, but the truth is that most people will never live this kind of life. We live lives of slavery to material possessions, instant gratification, popularity, and excessive consumption. All this is done in the name of being free and happy, but are we really living lives of freedom and happiness?

Stoicism teaches people to accept what they have in life so that you do not end up becoming a slave to their passions, desires, or emotions, whether positive or negative. Stoics believed that emotions are the cause of man's error in judgment, and it is, therefore, best to live in a way that is harmonious with nature. According to Stoics, the best way to determine a person's life philosophy is not through the words they speak but the way they behave.

The main goal of the Stoic philosophy is to lead man to a place of happiness through achieving what is known as "supreme ideal" or "virtue". There are four distinct qualities that make up this supreme ideal:

- Moral insight, also known as Wisdom

- Self-control

- Courage

- Justice

The objective of practicing virtue is to help a person achieve true self-sufficiency, and a life free from bad fortune or suffering. As a Stoic, it doesn't matter what your social status is in life. This is a personal characteristic that once achieved, allows you to live a life free from the shackles of this world.

Though Stoicism doesn't specifically make reference to God, it does talk about a Divine Will. However, the main emphasis is on people living together in a singular community enduring similar conditions and restraints. Your role as a Stoic would be to conform to the community by practicing two key duties:

## Accept your fate without complaining

Now, before you start assuming that this means being lazy or accepting negative circumstances in life, take note of this. Stoics believe in doing your best to improve your situation. Stoicism even recommends a life of public service and striving to improve your life. When we talk about accepting your fate without complaining, we mean choosing not to place too much significance on things that don't have permanent value.

One of the biggest challenges we face today is our inability to eliminate the distractions from our lives and focus on the things that truly matter. Somehow, we find ourselves constantly placing a high value on transient things such as money and possessions. A Stoic must always avoid getting fixated on unimportant things so that he can achieve true contentment and inner peace. If you learn to accept that in life, things come and go, you will be able to overcome the obstacles to inner peace and contentment. You will choose not to live a life that is based on greed, ambition, or luxury.

## Live according to nature's laws

When we talk about 'Nature's Laws' here, we are talking about going against conventional ways of living. Stoicism is essentially a philosophy that questions the status quo. For example, you should train yourself to live on the bare minimums of life. Learn how to survive on very little and plain food. Practice how to live with few items of clothing. Train yourself to live under basic shelter conditions. You don't have to do this throughout your entire life, but set aside a few days where you literally live on the bare necessities. The aim here is to see that there is really nothing to fear in living this kind of life. Most people work themselves to death, never spending time with their loved ones, as they claim to be working hard to provide a better life. In the end, all that hard work comes to nothing when you realize that it wasn't worth it.

Another idea for living according to nature's law is by developing your gift of reason. You should learn to overcome those crippling emotions that can devastate your life, such as fear (especially fear of dying), grief, anger, superstition, or pain. According to Stoic reasoning, there is no good or bad in this world because everything is a matter of perspective. In other words, rather than depend on your feelings as a source of truth, you should use your mind as the determining factor when discerning truth.

Now that we have a basic understanding of Stoicism, it is time to look at its origins. For this, we have to start by traveling way back in time.

## *Origins of Stoicism*

It's 300 B.C. and a man named Zeno, born in Cyprus, is sitting under a porch-like structure in Athens lecturing a group of other men on the principles of personal ethics. The men meet under the porch-like structure (which in Greek is referred to as *Stoa)* on a regular basis, and this is where the term Stoicism comes from. The term *Stoa Poikile* means "Painted Porch," and refers to where Zeno taught his philosophy.

Zeno didn't just stumble upon these Stoic principles. His lectures were actually influenced by Greek philosophers who preceded him, such as Socrates, Antisthenes, the Milesians, and Heracleitus of Ephesus. Zeno was able to learn the various philosophies and principles of these different schools of thought and used them as a basis for establishing the central Stoic doctrines.

What Zeno managed to do was divide Stoicism into three fundamental segments: Logic, Physics, and Ethics. He then infused the key Stoic principles into each of these parts, such that the Stoics who came onto the scene later were able to expand on his ideas without altering Zeno's foundation.

## *The Development of Stoicism*

Stoicism may have had its origins in Athens, but it soon spread across Greece and the Roman Empire. After the death of Aristotle and Alexander the Great, the Greek way of life changed, and the codes of conduct that people had become accustomed to were not suitable anymore. Athens was no longer the focus of world attention as Rome took up its cultural prominence.

The evolution of Stoicism is usually divided into three specific phases:

1. **Early Stoa**

This is during the early years of the Stoic school of thought (early to late 3rd century BCE) when Zeno and his doctrines were still flourishing. It is usually known as the era of early Greek Stoicism. It was during this period that the themes governing the fundamental framework of Stoicism were developed. After Zeno, the next head of the school of Stoics was Cleanthes of Assos, followed by Chrysippus of Soli. Chrysippus is considered the most prolific of the early Stoics due to his extraordinary devotion toward developing the three themes of logic, physics, and ethics.

## 2. Middle Stoa

This is the era of Roman Stoicism and includes the period between the 2nd and early 1st centuries BCE. At this point, Stoicism was being carried forward by the works of two Rhodes philosophers known as Panaetius and Poseidonius.

Panaetius ran a Stoic school in Rome while Poseidonius is known for highlighting the religious features of Stoicism. The Romans were known to be a practical people, and this meant that these two men had to convert the Stoic doctrine into morally philosophical themes that could help individuals on a personal level. They managed to break down Stoicism into practical steps, and thus these two men were the key reason why Stoicism became so popular in Rome.

## 3. Late Stoa

This is the period that includes the first two centuries CE. During this period, there were three figures that shaped the Stoic philosophy. One of them was Lucius Seneca, who was a Roman Statesman. There was Epictetus, who was an ex-slave. Finally, there was the Roman Emperor, Marcus Aurelius. These men spread the Stoic message at a time when Christianity was gaining ground across the world.

Unfortunately, the works of the philosophers of the first two phases did not survive, and what we are left with today are the Roman texts from the Late Stoa phase. As the centuries passed, Stoicism remained as one of the philosophies with the greatest impact in the Greco-Roman world. Though many people came after and modified it further, its basic principles managed to stay intact.

# Chapter 2:

# The Key Figures of Stoic Philosophy

So far we have covered a brief history of Stoicism as a philosophy, as well as some of its basic doctrines. In this chapter, we will learn more about some of the key figures that have defined Stoicism, both in the past and present era.

In modern times, the works of the Romans from the Late Stoa period has dominated Stoic literature. As we explained before, the written works of Stoics from the previous periods did not survive. Therefore, we shall be looking into the lives of Seneca, Epictetus, and Marcus Aurelius, and how they contributed to the Stoic philosophy. Finally, we shall also cover some modern Stoics you may recognize.

## *Seneca*

A joke is told of how men who possess genuine ability tend to take action, while the rest just spend their time philosophizing. This was a joke that was used to chide early philosophers for their excessive focus on philosophy rather than pursuing wealth. For Seneca, this was a personal issue because he was both a philosopher as well as a wealthy man. How was it possible for one of the wealthiest men in the Roman Empire to denounce riches as a negative thing? This was one of the paradoxes that made Seneca the most interesting Stoic who ever lived.

He was born Lucius Annaeus Seneca in Cordoba, Spain, around 4 B.C. He was the son of the well-known senator and writer Seneca the Elder. Seneca the Younger, as he was referred to, became active in politics and ended up as a prominent financial clerk. He also spent his time writing tragedies such as *Consolation to Maria*.

At around 41 A.D., he was exiled to the island of Corsica after being charged by Emperor Claudius for committing adultery with his niece, Julia Livilla. However, only eight years later, the emperor's wife, Agrippina, managed to convince Claudius to allow Seneca to return. She appointed him to become the tutor and adviser to her son, Nero, who would grow up to become one of the most tyrannical and notorious emperors in Roman history. This clearly cast a shadow over Seneca's character, considering that he made the bulk of his wealth while serving Nero.

Even though he faced many trials and tribulations during his life, Seneca stuck to the Stoic philosophy. His teacher and Stoic philosopher, Attalus, initially exposed him to this way of life. Cato, another renowned Stoic, also inspired Seneca. Seneca was not just a philosophical thinker. He was a doer as well. He navigated the ups and downs of life by remaining Stoic throughout. Even when Emperor Nero ordered him to kill himself for his alleged role in an assassination plot to kill the emperor, Seneca handled himself with dignity. He went from massive wealth to exile and back to wealth without losing his Stoic philosophical foundation.

Many renowned individuals have claimed Seneca to be a major influence over their lives. Notable figures like Pascal, Francis Bacon, Montaigne, Tim Ferris, and Nassim Taleb all refer to Seneca's teachings as having an impact on their lives.

What makes Seneca different from most other ancient philosophers is that his writings are more readable and enjoyable. This is probably because his works are in the form of letters. One of his works is known as *"On the Shortness of*

*Life*," and is a compilation of three letters that are stark reminders of how short life is and how wasteful we are with this precious, finite resource. Another one of his famous literary works is *Letters from a Stoic*, which is a guide on how to handle life issues such as grief, failure, success, poverty, anger, and many other things.

## Stoic Exercises from Seneca

Here are three exercises you can apply today, based on the life and works of Seneca the Younger:

### 1. Find your anchor

In his letters, Seneca advises us to choose role models who can provide us with a template to live our lives. Seneca pushes forth this idea because he believes a good role model will provide you with the right principles to help you navigate the tough times in life. Rather than get stuck not knowing how to handle a situation, a good role model will inspire you to take action as they did. Find someone whose character and way of life you approve of. As Seneca once said, without a ruler to measure yourself against, you cannot draw a straight line.

### 2. Don't become a slave to money

Seneca believed that philosophy and wealth did not have to be mutually exclusive. He wanted the benefits that a life of wealth brought but was never dependent on money. Seneca mastered his money instead of allowing it to enslave him. This should be a great lesson for people today who chase after wealth and end up becoming slaves to money.

According to Seneca, a wise man will take the gifts that good fortune brings his way without allowing his heart to be filled with love for material possessions. It is only fools who regard wealth as a master.

### 3. **Fight your ego**

Seneca recognized that your ego has the ability to block your learning and progress. If you examine today's society, everyone wants to be praised for everything they do. That is why you find people posting every intimate detail of their lives on social media, including what they had for lunch. The problem is that we gradually become accustomed to having our egos flattered and buy into our own hype, even when we know that these flatterers are lying. Look at some of the most tyrannical leaders we have in the world today. I'm sure every one of them believes that they are doing the right thing because the people around them are always praising them as they commit atrocities. Why would they even contemplate changing their evil behavior when their egos are already so inflated?

## *Epictetus*

One of the most captivating aspects of the Stoic philosophy is the fact that its three most famous practitioners came from such diverse backgrounds. While Seneca was a wealthy adviser to an emperor, and Marcus Aurelius was an emperor himself, Epictetus was born a slave. This shows the ability of Stoicism to transcend class barriers and provide people of diverse status with timeless principles for living.

Epictetus was born almost 2,000 years ago in Hierapolis, which is in present-day Turkey. He was a slave to a wealthy owner who allowed him to engage in liberal studies. This was how Epictetus ended up learning philosophy from his Stoic teacher, Musonius Rufus. After the death of Emperor Nero, Epictetus was set free and he began teaching philosophy in Rome. However, once Emperor Domitian ascended to the throne, all philosophers were banished, and Epictetus was forced to flee to Greece, where he taught philosophy until his death.

The teachings of Epictetus ended up becoming an influence to Marcus Aurelius, who would later mention him in his *Meditations*. Even James Stockdale, who was held as a prisoner of war for seven years in Vietnam credits the philosopher's teachings for helping him endure the tortures of imprisonment. Epictetus once lectured that sickness may hinder the body but not one's ability to choose; unless a person allowed it. For example, lameness may hinder your leg but not your ability to make decsions. He recommended that everyone who believes this principle will begin to see challenges of life as obstacles to other things or people, but not to oneself.

It is important to note that Epictetus never wrote any of his lectures down. The teachings we have today are the works of one of his students, Arrian, who wrote down his lectures in the form of notes. If you are just starting to learn Stoic principles and maxims, we recommend that you begin with Seneca or Marcus Aurelius. The reason is that most of Epictetus' teachings are difficult to read for beginners, and some of them are very long and require a greater commitment. For Epictetus, you can start with *Enchiridion* and then *Discourses*.

## Stoic Exercises from Epictetus

Here are three lessons you can apply today, based on the teachings of Epictetus:

### 1. Focus only on the things you can control

As a Stoic, one of the fundamental principles is to know how to distinguish between things within and outside your control. You should not allow yourself to be upset by people, situations, or events that you cannot influence. What you need to do is learn how to focus on your own actions and behavior. In other words, learn to let go and move forward with life despite the many challenges that plague us today.

### 2. Let your actions speak louder than your words

The problem with most people is that they constantly talk about what needs to be done but never get around to doing anything. Those who achieved the most in life have learned to take actions that set the standard for others to learn from. The best way to spend your energy isn't telling people how to live; it's actually living in a way that others are inspired by.

### 3. Set out a character and follow it

According to Epictetus, people are creatures of habit who falsely believe that character is set in stone and therefore cannot be changed. He challenged his students to prescribe themselves a character that they would like to have, and follow the principles necessary to attain that character. For example, if you want to develop self-confidence, then you have to start walking up to strangers and just saying hello. It may be difficult at first but every small step you take daily will lead you in the direction you want to go.

## Marcus Aurelius

Whenever we want to adopt a particular philosophy or principle of life, we tend to gravitate toward role models who have embraced those philosophies. This also applies to Stoicism as well. We need to ask ourselves who these people are and whether we should look up to them. With this regard, Marcus Aurelius definitely fits the bill.

First of all, Marcus Aurelius was not his birth name. He was actually born Marcus Annius Verus in 121 AD and grew up in a prominent family. Unfortunately, his father died when he was only three years old. As a young man, he liked serious sporting activities like hunting, boxing, and wrestling. No one would have believed that he would one day end up as emperor of Rome.

While he was a teenager, the emperor at that time, Hadrian, was a childless man who was on his deathbed. The person chosen to succeed him died suddenly, and Hadrian ended up settling on Antoninus Pius, the man who adopted Marcus Annius Verus as his son. That was how he ended up changing his name to Marcus Aurelius Antoninus.

Marcus took his education seriously and studied under renowned tutors such as Herodes Atticus and Marcus Cornelius Fronto. When he became emperor in 161 AD, he became one of the most powerful men of in the world, and such power would have afforded him anything he wanted. However, Marcus Aurelius was a believer in the Stoic philosophy, and this led him to adopt a sober approach to his way of ruling.

He managed to guide the Roman Empire using wisdom and virtue and even wrote his memoirs known as *Meditations*. He would write down ways of being more virtuous, wiser, more just, and more impervious to temptations. The stresses he dealt with on a daily basis would have overwhelmed him had it not been for the foundation of Stoicism he had learned during his youth. He thanked his teachers Rusticus as well as Epictetus and Heraclitus for influencing him to adopt Stoic thought.

His book, *Meditations*, was Marcus Aurelius' legacy to the world. However, it was never intended to be published because it was more of a personal diary. In the book, he talks about developing self-discipline, humility, strength, self-actualization, and personal ethics. These are all Stoic principles that helped him become one of the greatest emperors the Roman Empire had ever seen.

## Stoic Exercises from Marcus Aurelius

Here are three exercises you can apply today. They are based on the life and works of this great Stoic emperor.

### 1. **Practice those virtues that you can have**

Most often than not, we find ourselves looking at the natural abilities of others and envying their position. Instead of throwing a pity party, you can start practicing or maximizing the potential that is within you. For example, you may not be the smartest thinker or funniest person, but maybe you have the gift of patience, endurance, or honesty. Focus on these virtues instead.

## 2. Use the strength of others to keep you going

It is believed that Marcus Aurelius wrote some of his *Meditations* notes while he was fighting on the battlefield. During these difficult and adverse times, he would write encouraging notes to himself. He wrote how he would look at the troops around him and draw strength from their individual virtues, for example, one's generosity or modesty.

## 3. Focus on the present moment

In most cases, we find ourselves thinking and worrying about the past or future. We paint potential scenarios in our minds of all the negative things that may happen. The excuse behind this may be that you are preparing yourself for any potential outcome, but the reality is that you are allowing fear to set in and cripple you. Stoicism is about setting aside all kinds of emotions and focusing on what is in front of you right now. Don't focus on past events or potential future outcomes because they have no power over you. Restrict your mind to present limits. If your mind resists, then heap some shame on it.

## *Stoicism and Modern Culture*

In this section, I want to share a list of some people who have embraced this philosophy. You may be wondering whether the Stoic way of life is something that is right for you. Well, you may be inspired to read about how some of the most successful individuals and institutions have used these principles and doctrines to master themselves and enhance their perseverance and wisdom.

In today's world, Stoicism has become a way for some to enhance their stamina and strength to tackle life's challenges. Whether its football coaches, rappers, pro athletes, hedge fund managers, public officials, CEOs, or artists; Stoicism knows no bounds.

## In Politics:

Bill Clinton – Former US president who reads *Meditations* by Marcus Aurelius every year.

Thomas Jefferson – American founding father who kept a copy of Seneca's works on his nightstand.

Arnold Schwarzenegger – Former Mr. Olympia and California Governor who loves Stoic philosophy.

Wen Jiabao – Former Chinese Prime Minister who has read *Meditations* more than 100 times.

James Mattis – Present Defense Secretary who read *Meditations* while he was deployed overseas.

## In Pro Athletics:

Michael Lombardi – Renowned NFL executive who is credited with introducing Stoicism into football.

Tom Brady – Star quarterback for the New England Patriots who is inspired by Stoicism.

Nick Saban – University of Alabama head coach who uses the philosophies of Marcus Aurelius to prepare for football games.

Antonio Brown – The Pittsburg Steelers' NFL Pro Bowler who is inspired by Stoicism.

John Schneider – General Manager for the Settle Seahawks who was inspired by the Stoic book *The Obstacle is the Way*.


## In Music:

Twista – He mentioned Marcus Aurelius in one of his songs.

T-Pain - Has released a Stoic mixtape and album.

LL Cool J – He loves the book *The Obstacle is the Way*, which espouses the Stoic philosophy.

Lupe Fiasco – He mentioned Marcus Aurelius in one of his songs, *Lightwork*.


## Authors:

JK Rowling – The Harry Potter series author is inspired by Marcus Aurelius.

Robert Greene – Author of 48 Laws of Power who believes that Stoicism is a wonderful philosophy.

Nassim Taleb – Author and ex-trader who admires Seneca and Stoicism.

Ralph Waldo Emerson – This famous author incorporated Stoicism into some of his ideas.

## In Business:

Tim Ferris – Angel investor and author who has published Seneca's letters in the form of an audiobook.

Blake Irving – CEO of GoDaddy who has been motivated by *Obstacle is the Way*, a book inspired by Stoicism.

Jack Dorsey – Twitter co-founder who is a huge fan of Stoicism.

Kevin Rose – Renowned investor and entrepreneur who recommends *Ego is the Enemy*, a book inspired by Stoicism.

# Chapter 3:

# Understanding Stoic Principles

There are many principles and doctrines that have come out of the Stoic philosophy. This is due to the teachings of the different men who defined it and made it a way of life. Stoics were people who lived a realistic yet morally idealistic life. As the centuries have gone by, stretching from the Hellenistic period to the 21st century, Stoicism has not lost its practicality in dealing with the problems of life.

In this chapter, we will go a bit deeper into the principles, virtues, and disciplines that make Stoicism what it is today. Since this book is written for beginners looking to learn the basic tenets, the content has been simplified somewhat to ensure a thorough understanding of the philosophy.

## The Three Topoi

When learning about Stoicism, you must first begin by understanding what is known as *the Three Topoi*, which we mentioned when discussing the origins of the philosophy. The three topoi are logic, physics, and ethics. They are connected to the *Four Virtues* and *Three Disciplines*, which we shall talk about later on.

The three topoi are considered to be areas of inquiry that provide the foundation for the whole Stoic philosophical system. They were first identified by Zeno, and can be further broken down as follows:

- The Logic – Modern logic proper, epistemology, rhetoric, and cognitive science

- The Physics – Modern natural science, theology, and metaphysics

- The Ethics – The best ways of living one's life

These three parts are supposed to blend into one another and are taught together. According to Zeno and Chrysippus, two of the earliest Stoics, they are meant to follow a specific sequence when being taught, that is, the logic first, then physics, and finally ethics. In order to better understand this sequence, visualize a garden surrounded by a fence.

Logic represents the fence and is studied first because it provides you with the tools required for sound reasoning. Without logic, it will be impossible to understand the next two topoi. Physics is represented by the fertile soil in the garden. It helps us understand how the world and human nature work. Finally, ethics is the crop that grows out of the soil. Once you figure out how to best live your life, the result will be your personal ethics.

## The Three Disciplines

Epictetus defined three key disciplines that every Stoic student needs to practice. They are:

- Desire – This first discipline covers both your desires and aversions. In other words, there are certain things that you should aim for and others that you should stay away from. According to Stoic philosophy, you should only desire things that are under your complete control because you are sure of getting them. These include sound judgment and good behavior.

Those things that are beyond your complete control, such as wealth and fame, should not be desired.

- Action – This discipline relates to the way you behave toward other people. As you engage in various activities, you should always act in an orderly and reasonable manner. This means you should not behave carelessly.

- Assent – This covers freedom from being deceived or making irrational decisions. At any given time, you receive many different signals or impressions from the world around you. In most cases, we jump to irrational conclusions before our brain even kicks in. Let's say you are walking down the street at night and hear a rustling sound from the bushes by the side of the road. You are likely to become tense, or even move away due to fear. However, once your rational mind examines the situation, you realize it was just a kitten. Therefore, your initial impression of possible danger was wrong, and you need to withdraw assent from that decision.

According to Epictetus, the most important of these three disciplines was desire. His reasoning was that man usually suffers from anxieties, sorrow, bad luck, and jealousy simply because he constantly desires things. When you fail to obtain what you desire, you start experiencing negative emotions, and this makes you too stubborn to be reasonable. This is what happens when you want things that are outside your control.

You need to have the right perspective here. This does not mean you should not allow yourself to have any desires at all. However, whenever you want something, always make sure that your actions are reasonable and do not harm your natural relationships with others. This is how the first and second disciplines are linked. The third discipline is crucial if progress is to be made in the first two. It simply makes sure that even in situations where you do not have any active desires or actions (e.g. when sleeping or drunk), nothing catches you off guard.

## The Four Virtues

There are four virtues that a Stoic must possess. These virtues are sometimes also referred to as the four unifying principles. They are given this name because they are the link between the three topoi and the three disciplines explained above. The four virtues are:

- Courage

- Temperance (Self-control)

- Justice

- Wisdom (prudence, mindfulness)

In order to understand and practice Stoicism as a way of life, it is important to see how all these different elements come together.

Physics is linked to Desire through the virtues of Courage and Self-control. We desire things because we are able to understand how the world around us works, which is a function of physics. The virtues of courage (ability to accept things as they are) and self-control (not desiring things you cannot have) help to mediate between physics and desire.

Ethics and Action are linked through the virtue of Justice. Whenever a Stoic takes a specific action, they should make sure that their behavior does not harm others (ethical). This is only possible if they practice and embrace the virtue of justice.

Finally, Logic is linked to Assent through the virtue of Wisdom. As a Stoic who is constantly bombarded with various impressions from their surrounding environment, it is important that you use reason to either grant or refuse assent to an impression. To do so requires that you maintain the virtue of wisdom.

The Three Topoi, the Three Disciplines, and the Four Virtues are all interconnected in some way, and for you to practice one set, you will need to embrace the others as well. If you look at the above system and how everything seamlessly links to another, it is clear to see that Stoicism as a philosophy is actually quite relevant in today's world.

## *Stoic Principles*

There are eight general principles that reflect the philosophy of Stoicism. These principles have been adapted into many of today's popular wisdom. For example, some of them are part of the Serenity Prayer while others can be seen in most Twelve-Step programs.

Here are the eight Stoic principles:

1.  Nature – Nature is based on reason.

2.  Law of Reason – This law governs the entire Universe. Since humans cannot escape this law, they have to follow it in their own unique ways.

3. Virtue – If you live according to rational nature, your life will be virtuous.

4. Wisdom – This is considered to be the root of all other virtues. Once you learn to practice wisdom, you will gain a sense of justice, self-control, and courage.

5. Apatheia – For a Stoic, all kinds of passion are irrational and must be avoided. You should avoid any kind of intense feelings.

6. Pleasure – Pleasure is regarded as neither good nor bad, as long as you do not allow it to become an obstacle in your quest for virtue.

7. Evil – There is no evil in being poor, sick, or dying.

8. Duty – You should not pursue a virtuous life simply out of a desire for pleasure. You should do it out of a sense of duty.

All these principles are part of Stoic ethical doctrine, where the goal is to avoid intense *passion*. Stoics believe that having intense passion will only lead to anguish and suffering. As a result, Stoicism advocates for the pursuit of *reason* and *apatheia* as a way to become unemotional and have clear judgment. If you can stay indifferent to all the external events, and choose to be passive regardless of whether life is good or bad, you will live a better life.

This seems practical especially in today's world where you are very happy one day and miserable the next. The news is constantly full of sad and worrying headlines, and if you are the type who is sensitive to situations, you can quickly find yourself feeling anxious and stressed out. Stoics do not see events as being evil or good, and life must simply go on.

# Chapter 4:

# Stoicism & Emotional Control

There is a misconception out there that a Stoic does not feel. It is important to be clear right now that the Stoic way of life is not about repressing your emotions. In actual fact, Stoics believe that if you live life well, you will experience joy and tranquility. Stoics should not be viewed as robots who do not feel anything. In contrast, Stoicism is about learning what it means to be human. The Stoic motto states that humans must *live according to nature*, which means that the primary emphasis is on learning to fit into the universe.

Living in the world today involves dealing with many strange and messy interactions that elicit a range of emotions. For Stoics, there is greater emphasis placed on the mind, rather than pandering to unstable emotions. In other words, if you want to be a Stoic, you must learn how to control your emotions and not allow them to define your life.

## *The Emotional Stoic*

We want you to see Stoicism as a way of approaching your emotional life in a distinct manner. For example, rather than allowing emotions to guide your behavior, treat them like you would the weather. Let's say you are leaving for work in the morning and it starts to rain. You may be forced to grab an umbrella or drive your car slower than normal, but ultimately you still have to get to work. This is how you should handle your emotions.

Just go ahead and feel the negative emotion, be it anger, fear, or grief, and then choose to act as if all is well. Imagine a person who is angry and starts being rude to their colleagues at work. This person, when challenged about their behavior, would use the excuse of anger to justify their actions. The question is, would you agree with that excuse or not? The funny thing is that the majority would allow that person to get away with it because we also behave in the same manner all the time.

We have created a culture where it is permissible to *behave badly* because you *feel bad*. This is what Stoicism is against. A Stoic believes that it is utter nonsense to behave or talk negatively to others just because you are experiencing a negative emotion. There are two lessons that you need to learn here. Firstly, according to the Stoic philosophy, such a person is angry because they have adopted a negative perspective of their situation. It is not the emotion that is the problem, but rather the response. Secondly, the person can still choose to act virtuously despite what they are feeling.

As you can see, Stoicism is not about hiding your emotions or suppressing them. Go ahead and feel what you want to feel, just as long as you don't make decisions according to those emotions.

## Passions versus the Good States

As a student of Stoic ethics, one thing that you must have understood by now is that passions are irrational. In other words, being controlled by your passions and desires will hinder you from living a life of virtue. This is why one of the eight principles of the Stoic philosophy is *Apathy,* which means indifference or lack of passion.

For a Stoic, the only good thing in life is *virtue*, and therefore, all manner of vices must be avoided. This is one area that tends to confuse most people. We usually categorize events and objects to be either good or bad, yet in most cases, they are actually indifferent. This tendency to judge something in an irrational or unreasonable way is what Stoics refer to as *pathos* or passion. In Stoic philosophy, passions are regarded as the "bad feelings," and should not be present in the soul of a virtuous person.

There are four types of passions in Stoicism. These are Pleasure, Appetite, Distress, and Fear. Just to clarify, pleasure and distress are related to present objects while appetite and fear are linked to future objects. Let's try to unpack these passions further so that we understand them better.

Pleasure is an irrational craving for something that is present, transient and outside your control. A good example would be rejoicing at the misfortune of others. Appetite is more future oriented and describes an irrational pursuit of a good expectation. Great examples would be greed, revenge, intense sexual desire, and hatred. Distress refers to the irrational contraction of your soul and includes malice, grief, jealousy, worry, anguish, and stress. Fear is the irrational shrinking of your soul with the expectation that something bad will happen in the future. Examples include agony, shame, superstition, and terror.

On the other hand, there are also "good feelings" in Stoicism, which every virtuous person should possess. These are referred to as the *three affective responses* or *good states*. They are Joy, Caution, and Wish. Joy is considered to be the opposite of pleasure and is described as a rational excitement, such as tranquility and being in good spirits.

Caution is the opposite of fear and is a rational avoidance of something that may bring harm in the future. Examples of caution would be sanctity and respect. Wish is the opposite of appetite, and is the rational striving to achieve something in the future, for example, contentment, acceptance, or goodwill. Distress is the only bad feeling that has no opposite.

Here is an example of Joy versus Pleasure to wrap this all up:

If you are a virtuous person, you will experience joy when hanging out with your best friend. However, the presence of your friend is not in itself as good as having virtue. In other words, though you prefer being around them, you won't do so at the expense of other responsibilities. Even when they are absent, you will still be in good spirits.

For a person who is not virtuous, things are very much different. A "vicious" person allows their soul to be gripped by pleasure, and they may run around seeking material riches. When that wealth is gone, the vicious person is immediately plagued by an irrational fear of poverty, and they become miserable.

From all this, it is clear to see that Stoics are not cold or unfeeling people, but rather rational people who know how to control their emotions. If an event brings joy, that is great, but if the event doesn't occur, then there is no disappointment either. Stoics are not passionless statues, but people who are mindful of the difference between the things that bring happiness (virtues) and those that do not (vices). Stoicism ensures a firm and consistent way of life where the ups and downs don't end up stirring your passions.

# Chapter 5:

# Stoicism & Relationships

What does Stoicism say about relationships? At first glance, it may appear that a Stoic will find it very difficult to maintain proper relationships with others. However, we have seen in the previous chapter that a Stoic is not devoid of emotions. Stoicism simply embraces the rational use of emotions without necessarily succumbing to their control.

## *Stoicism, Love, and Friendships*

Here are a few points to ponder about Stoicism and its relation to love and friendship:

1. Stoicism does not mean you have to be unemotional in your relationships. The truth is that this philosophy emphasizes the idea of natural affection.

2. Stoics were one of the first philosophical schools to promote the incorporation of women as philosophers. Stoicism was even taught to both men and women as a way of helping people maintain a philosophical perspective toward family and children.

3. Stoicism encourages us to not only love ourselves but to go further and love all others. As a Stoic, you should expand your natural affection for yourself toward your family, and then humanity at large. You should become a lover of humanity or a philanthropist.

4. Stoicism encourages us to love nature and God by peacefully accepting situations or events that are beyond our control. Whatever happens in life,

especially things that you didn't see coming, just accept it as a part of life and move on.

5.  For a Stoic, it is wrong to be unnaturally or irrationally attached to another person. The best way to truly love someone or something is by accepting that nothing in this life is permanent. This will help you love people without placing unnecessary expectations on them to make you happy. Love others but realize that some things are beyond your control and can change at any moment.

6.  Stoicism teaches that the love you show others is more valuable than the love others give back to you. It is more virtuous to show friendship than to receive it. This may seem out of place in our modern world, but the reasoning behind it is remarkable. A Stoic should always believe that the wisdom and strength that is within their personal character is more valuable than the manner in which they are treated by others. People may criticize and mistreat you, but this does not affect your personal character. You have to learn to be strong and wise in your response.

## *Natural Affection*

The teachings of Epictetus are recorded in a book known as *Discourses*. In this book, there is a chapter that highlights natural or family affection. This example will help you further understand how Stoicism views relationships.

One day, a man came to see Epictetus about his miserable married life. Epictetus told the man that marriage and children were meant to bring happiness rather than misery, so clearly, there was something wrong somewhere. The man explained that when his young daughter had recently fallen sick and was on the verge of death, he had been overwhelmed with grief. Consequently, he had run away from the house for a couple of days. He was only able to return after he received word that she had fully recovered. According to the distressed father, this was a natural reaction because any dad would be distressed by such a frightening ordeal.

Being the Stoic that he is, Epictetus told the man that things done according to nature are right, but questioned whether running away was the most natural reaction. The Stoic motto states that if you live according to nature, you will always take the right actions. While it was true that most fathers would want to flee such a situation, the question still remained as to whether that would ultimately be the right thing to do.

Epictetus noted that when an event occurs, there are certain reactions that are popular, but we should never assume that what is popular is automatically the natural response. What is common and what is natural are very different. So Epictetus asked the man if he had criteria for determining whether a specific action was natural or not. Not surprisingly, the man did not. To Epictetus, failing to have criteria for knowing what is natural is the greatest harm that can happen to a person. He, therefore, recommended that the man discovers his own criteria for judging every individual case in his life.

But since the man needed immediate advice, Epictetus asked him whether having affection for his family was natural and morally good. The man answered positively. Furthermore, they both agreed that whatever is rational with regard to life is also morally good. However, there was a conundrum. If family affection is good, and rational living is also good, then they shouldn't be a contradiction between the two. If the man says that he loves his family, and insists that his decision to run away was rational, why is he miserable then?

The bottom line is that family affection and living rationally are both good, but the man's *decision* to flee from his child's bedside was not rational. He may think that it was an expression of his great love for his daughter, but it was not the natural or morally right thing to do. Would it have been rational if the mother had done the same thing? What if he had been on his deathbed and his family ran away? Would he agree that their love was so great that they just had to flee from him?

Using this debating technique known as *reduction ad absurdum*, Epictetus was able to help the man recognize how contradictory and silly his excuse was. The decision to flee was not due to his natural affection but a form of avoidance. He was trying to escape a painful situation.

This is what Stoicism teaches us about natural affection and relationships with others. You should not allow external events to dictate your relationships with others. When you decide that you don't love someone anymore and want to end a relationship, it's always easy to look for an external event to use as an excuse. The truth is that you made a conscious decision based on your opinion. Just because it is the popular thing to do doesn't make it the natural or morally right action.

The lesson is to stop blaming external events that are beyond your control and start taking responsibility for your choices. This is the Stoic way of life. Learn to study your decisions and identify whether they are natural or morally good.

# Chapter 6:

# Handling Failure like a Stoic

Everyone who has ever started some kind of venture or project has hoped or expected to succeed. Even if it was sitting an exam, you probably walked into that room aiming to pass. When you start a new relationship, you are usually hoping that he or she might be the one. But what happens when all your best-laid plans don't work out the way you thought they would? Do you break down with disappointment? Do you allow your emotions to overwhelm you and take out your frustrations on others? How would a Stoic handle failure?

## *Responding to Failure*

Seneca once wrote that there is nothing that happens to a wise man contrary to his expectation. In other words, he was trying to say that a person who espouses the virtue of wisdom is never surprised by the outcome of any situation or event.

As a Stoic, you should never be surprised when you fail at something. This is how to respond to failure. The biggest reason why most people are devastated by their failures in life is that they never considered that the outcome could be anything other than what they wanted. These failures can be both big (trying to get your business off the ground) or small (trying to get to a meeting but getting stuck in traffic). As long as your expectations are not met, you will feel frustrated.

The Stoics handled failure by using a technique known as *negative visualization*. They practiced this by spending a lot of time meditating on all the potential negative outcomes, worst case scenarios, and things that would be beyond their control. This may seem strange and depressing to some, but the goal was to eliminate the frustration that comes with negative surprises. It is a way of doing something with your eyes open so that you know how to adjust or prevent potential failure.

Stoics believed that you needed to be wise in all endeavors, so you had to be aware of every possibility and prepare for it. If you do this, failure will not be in your vocabulary because whatever goes wrong will simply be an outcome like any other.

According to Marcus Aurelius, a Stoic responds to an unpleasant outcome by making the most of it. Whatever obstacles may be in your way are meant to motivate you to take further action. Every success or failure is supposed to be an opportunity to apply a virtue. For example, getting stuck in traffic is an opportunity to learn patience and accept that some things are not within your control. If someone is rude toward you, take that as a chance to act the right way even if you don't feel like it. A failed business could be an opportunity to teach budding entrepreneurs some of the mistakes to avoid.

This is how Stoics handle failure. They learn to see every misfortune as another opportunity to learn something, do something better, or reevaluate. This is not a philosophy that you learn in one day. It takes a lifetime of taking every situation in your stride as you learn from your mistakes and failures.

Keep asking yourself how each specific failure is going to take you to the next level. It may be heart-wrenching at first, but you have to try. Once you start seeing failure with this new perspective, it won't be long before it becomes instinctive. People around you will start wondering why you always seem to overcome obstacles without breaking down. The Stoic philosophy can elevate you to a level where failure ultimately leads to more and more success.

# Chapter 7:

## Stoicism in the 21st Century

Some people aren't very fond of anything that has the philosophy tag on it. They think that such things are just mere abstract talk and aren't really practical for 21st-century living. However, Stoicism is still very practical in our modern lives.

When you look at the movers and shakers of today's world, it is easy to assume that they became successful due to expertise, talent, passion, or perseverance alone. While all these things may have contributed to their success, it is important to recognize the role played by the principles that guide their mind and behavior. How did they handle failure before they succeeded? How did they motivate themselves? In other words, what philosophy do they live by?

With all the trials and tribulations around us, we need a philosophy that teaches us how to live better lives as humans and overcome these challenges. Regardless of your professional or financial status, Stoic principles are still relevant and practical to your life today. As a 21st century Stoic, you should focus on two main things:

- How to lead a happy and fulfilled life

- How to become a better person

In this concluding chapter, we are going to take the principles of Stoicism and try to adapt them to real-life situations. If you embrace and practice these principles on a regular basis, you will be able to become a better worker, boost your creativity, and enhance your general state of mind. If you live and work without a guiding philosophy, you will always find yourself succumbing to distractions and excuses. You will simply find it easier to follow your moods rather than your principles.

## 8 Stoic Principles for Today's Society

### 1. Stop procrastinating

This is a big problem for most people. Your alarm goes off and you immediately hit the Snooze button. You've got important things to accomplish but you'd rather watch Netflix. Marcus Aurelius wrote in *Meditations* that humans should not complain when they are required to wake up early and go to work. We were not created to stay warm under the covers and sleep all day. If animals, birds, and insects are always busy doing their tasks without fail, humans should also live according to nature and do what nature demands. In other words, do what you were called to do, and stop putting off important stuff.

### 2. Be brutally honest with yourself

We all have some bad habits that we need to get rid of, but how many people actually admit that? Self-awareness is one of the first steps in changing your habits for the better. If you skipped work to sleep and watch movies then it's time to investigate why you behave this way. Of course, you will face some internal resistance, but that is the signal that you need to keep digging deeper. According to Seneca, a person who is not even aware of their wrongdoing is unlikely to act right. You have to be totally honest with yourself if you want to change your life.

### 3. **Accept that all your emotions come from inside you**

Marcus Aurelius said that he was able to discard and escape from anxiety because the emotion was within him, and not outside. This means that you always have the ability to control your emotions. If you have a long to-do list or an impending deadline, the problem isn't the workload in front of you. It is the way you think about the workload that creates negative feelings. Instead of finding an excuse not to get the work done, or blaming something external, recognize that the battle is in your mind. Look within yourself and deal with it.

### 4. **Find a role model**

Seneca believed in the importance of using a role model as a standard for your life. You may be a writer, artist, designer, or entrepreneur who is just starting out. What you need to do is get access to other professionals who are in your field and study their life, work, successes, and failures. This is possible especially through the internet. There is always somebody you can learn from. Even if you don't gain the same success as they do, continue to learn and grow.

### 5. **Stop responding to insignificant things in life**

Marcus Aurelius once said that you are better off not wasting valuable time on small things. We all know that social media has become like a microcosm of society, where people from all over the world interact. However, this can sometimes be a negative thing, especially when you are dealing with people who are intent on making your life miserable. For example, some people derive pleasure from trolling others and insulting them. Instead of engaging in some online war, choose to ignore these people. Stop wasting time staring at other people's photos when you should be attending to more important tasks.

## 6. Realize that failure is not the end of life

Have you ever completed a project after working hard for weeks or months, and then people criticize or ignore it? For most people, this may be a big blow to their ego, and they may react in a negative way. However, Stoicism requires that you endure and prevail over whatever pain that may come upon you. Failure is never the end of the road. You have to learn from the experience and recover from your setback. Without failure, there is no growth.

## 7. Apply the knowledge that you have acquired from books

Epictetus said that reading books is never enough. You have to prove that you have gained insight from that knowledge, and are now more reflective and discerning. It is one thing to internalize the contents of a book and quite another to make use of that information. You may be reading this book on Stoic philosophy right now, but are you going to apply these principles to your life? Reading that marketing or engineering book will help prepare your mind, but ultimately there has to be a physical manifestation of that action. In the end, you should take some kind of action that leads to success, failure, lessons learned, or an increase in wisdom.

## 8. Stop getting distracted by your phone

Seneca said that the true measure of a well-ordered mind is the ability to stop what you are doing and just be present. We live in a world filled with all kinds of distractions, especially our digital devices. We rarely spend any time establishing meaningful connections in real life because we have forgotten how to be present and mindful of the moment. There are people who can't even think of spending time alone without their phone. You need to take some time and just sit somewhere quiet, switch off your phone, and just take deep breaths. If you are working, focus fully on what you are doing. If you learn to be present, you will improve your quality of life.

Stoicism is very much an asset in everyday life. It imparts helpful teachings that have immediate practical value even in the 21st century. This philosophy is not just another bunch of archaic or extravagant metaphors that don't work. Learn these principles and apply them daily, and you will be amazed at just how effective they are in transforming your life!

# Conclusion

Stoicism is not just another philosophy that has great theories but cannot be applied practically. It is a way of life that can help you deal with everyday life issues, especially in this world that appears to be out of control. With all the economic crises, political turmoil, and disruptions that plague our society, the Stoic philosophy is one of the best ways to deal with obstacles in an honorable and virtuous way.

We hope that this book has taught you how to make the best of your life, no matter what happens. You should use Stoicism as a general philosophy to guide the decisions you make every day. Learn to rely less on your emotions and more on the virtues and disciplines of Stoicism.

If you succeed, be proud but not filled with pride. If you fail, take it in stride and learn from the experience. At the end of the day, whatever you do, always remember to live according to nature!

# Resources

www.dailystoic.com

www.thoughtco.com

www.modernstoicism.com

www.howtobeastoic.com

www.99u.com

www.philosophybasics.com

www.ieu.utm.edu

www.immoderatestoic.com

**Thank you once again for ordering this book!**

I truly hope you found value and inspiration in it. If you enjoyed Stoicism, found it useful or otherwise, I'd really appreciate it if you could post a short review on Amazon. Reviews are *gold* for authors and I do read all of them personally, so that I can continually write what people are wanting.

Visit the link below to leave a review:

## www.amazon.com/dp/B073ZY822T

Many thanks & best wishes,
*Elizabeth*

# Bonus!

As a way of saying thank you, I'd like to offer you another whole eBook *completely free of charge.* This free book is an essential beginner's guide to Practical Personal Development. It is my compilation of the most popular self development concepts around today and includes a ton of useful tips you can work into your everyday life.

You will also be the first to get notified of new book releases and special offers!

Simply visit the link below:

## www.goo.gl/4KgGsb

Made in the USA
Middletown, DE
19 August 2018